Questions and Answers About
ELLIS ISLAND

MYRNA NAU

PowerKiDS
press™

NEW YORK

Published in 2019 by The Rosen Publishing Group, Inc.
29 East 21st Street, New York, NY 10010

First Edition

Editor: Elizabeth Krajnik
Book Design: Michael Flynn

Photo Credits: Cover, pp. 9, 24 Courtesy of the Library of Congress; cover, pp. 1, 3–10, 12–14, 16, 18–22, 24–32 (background texture) NuConcept Dezine/Shutterstock.com; p. 5 Edwin Levick/Hulton Archive/Getty Images; p. 6 iofoto/Shutterstock.com; p. 7 North Wind Picture Archives; p. 11 Geography Photos/Universal Images Group/Getty Images; p. 13 (top) https://commons.wikimedia.org/wiki/File:Ellis_Island_First_Bldg_Burnt_15-June-1897.jpg; p. 13 (bottom) MPI/Stringer/Archive Photos/Getty Images; pp. 15, 17 Courtesy of the National Park Service, Statue of Liberty National Monument; p. 18 Courtesy of the Statue of Liberty-Ellis Island Foundation, Inc.; pp. 19, 21 (bottom), 23 Bettmann/Getty Images; p. 21 (top) Jacob A. Riis/Archive Photos/Getty Images; p. 25 Bain News Service/Buyenlarge/Archive Photos/Getty Images; p. 26 Courtesy of the New York Public Library; p. 27 Ian Ference/Barcroft Media/Landov; p. 29 Records of the U.S. House of Representatives, National Archives and Records Administration.

Cataloging-in-Publication Data

Names: Nau, Myrna.
Title: Questions and answers about Ellis Island / Myrna Nau.
Description: New York : PowerKids Press, 2019. | Series: Eye on historical sources | Includes glossary and index.
Identifiers: LCCN ISBN 9781538341124 (pbk.) | ISBN 9781538341117 (library bound) | ISBN 9781538341131 (6 pack)
Subjects: LCSH: Ellis Island Immigration Station (N.Y. and N.J.)–Juvenile literature. | Ellis Island (N.J. and N.Y.)–History–Juvenile literature. | United States–Emigration and immigration–Juvenile literature.
Classification: LCC JV6484.N38 2019 | DDC 304.8'73–dc23

Manufactured in the United States of America

CPSIA Compliance Information: Batch #CS18PK: For Further Information contact Rosen Publishing, New York, New York at 1-800-237-9932

CONTENTS

WELCOME TO THE UNITED STATES

Ellis Island, a tiny island in New York Harbor, was one of the first pieces of American land more than 12 million **immigrants** stood on when coming to the United States. Ellis Island operated as an immigration station from 1892 to 1954. In that time, it became one of the most-used immigration stations in the country.

Immigration plays a very important part in American history. Most American citizens have family members who immigrated many years ago—some as far back as colonial times. Without immigration, the United States would never have been established. Today, Ellis Island serves as an immigration museum, which helps visitors understand how our **diverse** nation came to be by telling the stories of the people who crossed an ocean to settle here.

Sources from the Past

Quoted below is part of Emma Lazarus's poem "The New Colossus," which was put onto a bronze plaque and hung on the inner wall of the Statue of Liberty's base:

> Give me your tired, your poor,
> Your huddled [gathered] masses yearning [longing] to breathe free,
> The wretched [rotten] refuse [garbage] of your teeming [crowded] shore.
> Send these, the homeless, tempest [storm]-tost to me,
> I lift my lamp beside the golden door!

Lazarus wrote this poem in 1883 to help raise money for the statue's base. The plaque was installed on the base in 1903. "The New Colossus" is a primary source and can help us gain a better understanding of the era of immigration during which the Statue of Liberty was created.

MANY OF THE IMMIGRANTS THAT CAME THROUGH ELLIS ISLAND WERE FROM EUROPE. UPON ARRIVAL, THEY SAW THE STATUE OF LIBERTY, WHICH FRANCE GAVE TO THE UNITED STATES IN THE 1880S. THE STATUE OF LIBERTY SITS ON LIBERTY ISLAND, WHICH USED TO BE CALLED BEDLOE'S ISLAND.

THE ISLAND'S HISTORY

Over the course of its early history, the island went by a number of different names, including Dyre's Island, Bucking Island, Gibbet Island, and Oyster Island. It earned the name Ellis Island after Samuel Ellis purchased it sometime before 1785. After Ellis died in 1794, the island was passed from one family member to another for about ten years.

ELLIS ISLAND TODAY

IN 1835, THE U.S. NAVY PUT A GUNPOWDER STORAGE BUILDING ON ELLIS ISLAND. DURING THE CIVIL WAR, THE AMOUNT OF WEAPONS AND GUNPOWDER GREW. AT THE END OF THE WAR, MANY PEOPLE WERE CONCERNED ABOUT HAVING SUCH A LARGE QUANTITY OF EXPLOSIVES SO CLOSE TO NEW YORK CITY AND JERSEY CITY, NEW JERSEY.

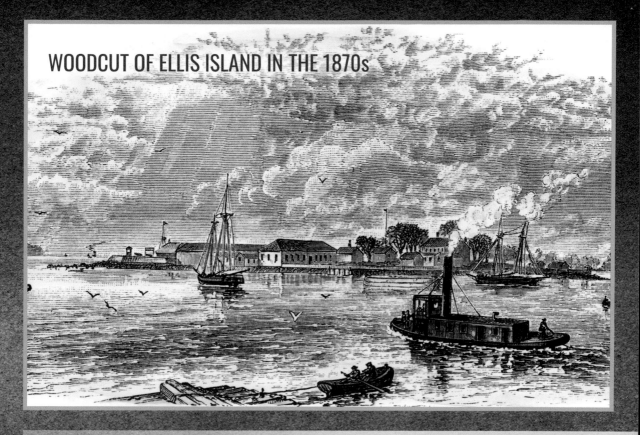

WOODCUT OF ELLIS ISLAND IN THE 1870s

Ellis Island, although privately owned, became home to an army battery, or two or more big military guns that are controlled as a unit. The battery was used to protect New York Harbor in the years before the War of 1812. In 1807, the state of New York purchased Ellis Island for military purposes and legally gave ownership of it to the federal government the next year. During the War of 1812, Ellis Island supported a small military post, but saw no active fighting.

CHANGES IN IMMIGRATION

In 1875, the federal government began taking a more active role in controlling and overseeing immigration. New laws were put in place to keep certain people, such as criminals and people believed to be taking jobs from American workers, out of the United States.

The U.S. government created a federally structured immigration system, which was headed by the secretary of the U.S. Treasury, to make sure the immigration process went smoothly. However, state workers at the Castle Garden immigration station weren't obeying the law, so federal workers were sent there to keep an eye on things.

The inspectors, or people whose job it is to look at immigrants carefully, at Castle Garden were accused of **abusing** immigrants, stealing money from them, and allowing unfit immigrants into the country. The federal government soon took control of processing immigrants at Castle Garden.

BEFORE ELLIS ISLAND WAS TURNED INTO AN IMMIGRATION STATION, MOST IMMIGRANTS COMING INTO THE UNITED STATES FROM EUROPE WERE PROCESSED THROUGH CASTLE GARDEN IN LOWER MANHATTAN.

Sources from the Past

Illustrations such as the one pictured here are considered primary sources because they were created at the same time history was being created. If a drawing were made based off this one, that drawing wouldn't be considered a primary source because it was created after the time period of study. Do you think this illustration is valuable to study? Why or why not?

A NEW LIFE FOR ELLIS ISLAND

One of the government's first orders of business was to build an immigration station in New York City large enough to handle the ever-increasing number of immigrants coming to America through New York Harbor. The treasury secretary's first idea was to use Bedloe's Island. However, the public didn't like this idea because Bedloe's Island was the site of the Statue of Liberty. Congress looked into the issue and decided to make Ellis Island the main gateway to America.

In 1890, the New York immigration station at Castle Garden closed. Construction began at Ellis Island in spring 1890 and was completed in January 1892. The final construction included a large two-story main building, separate hospital buildings, a laundry building, bathhouses, and an electric plant, all of which were made of wood.

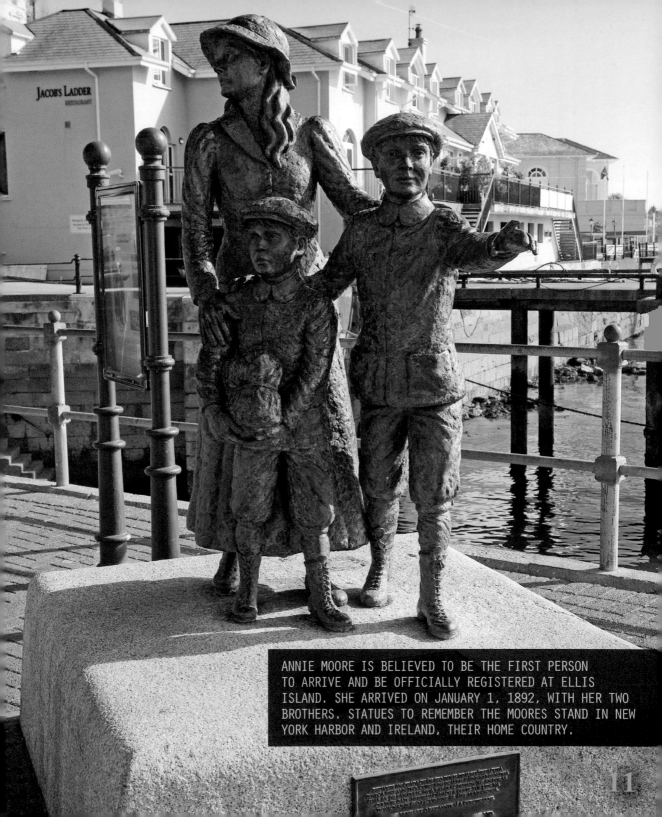

ANNIE MOORE IS BELIEVED TO BE THE FIRST PERSON
TO ARRIVE AND BE OFFICIALLY REGISTERED AT ELLIS
ISLAND. SHE ARRIVED ON JANUARY 1, 1892, WITH HER TWO
BROTHERS. STATUES TO REMEMBER THE MOORES STAND IN NEW
YORK HARBOR AND IRELAND, THEIR HOME COUNTRY.

11

PROBLEMS AT ELLIS ISLAND

Certain groups of people soon became the targets, or objects, of **prejudice** at Ellis Island. These immigrants were known as the "undesirable element" or unwanted people—a term that applied to Hungarians, Lithuanians, Russians, and Italians. Northern Europeans who had already established themselves in the United States feared these new immigrants would be willing to work for less money than they were. People suffering from certain diseases, or sicknesses, also weren't allowed into the United States.

In the first five years, immigration steadily declined, or lessened—partly due to an outbreak of **cholera** in Europe. On June 15, 1897, a fire completely destroyed the compound at Ellis Island. Immigration records stating the arrival of hundreds of thousands of immigrants in New York from 1855 to 1897 were lost. A month later, construction began on a new, more fireproof station at Ellis Island.

OLD IMMIGRATION STATION

NEW IMMIGRATION STATION

THE NEW IMMIGRATION STATION WAS COMPLETED IN 1900 FOR A TOTAL OF $1.5 MILLION. THAT'S ABOUT $41.4 MILLION IN TODAY'S MONEY.

CORRUPTION AND REFORM

Even though the immigration station at Ellis Island was rebuilt, corrupt, or dishonest, inspectors and staff continued to cause problems at the new station. Accusations quickly resurfaced that immigrants were being robbed, cheated out of money, and abused by station staff. Steamship captains and immigration inspectors were selling U.S. citizenship papers to newly arrived immigrants, allowing them to skip inspection at Ellis Island.

In 1901, President Theodore Roosevelt set about reforming, or improving, immigration practices at Ellis Island by hiring a new commissioner of immigration—William Williams. Williams introduced immigration reform at Ellis Island during one of the largest immigration waves in American history. Williams insisted, or strongly urged, the inspectors treat all immigrants with fairness and kindness. His guidelines were continued by Robert Watchorn, who was the commissioner after Williams.

THEODORE ROOSEVELT SUPPORTED LIMITING THE AMOUNT OF IMMIGRATION, BUT IN A KIND AND FAIR WAY. HE HAD A CLOSE RELATIONSHIP WITH IMMIGRANTS AND TRUSTED THEM TO HOLD IMPORTANT ROLES IN SOCIETY.

THEODORE ROOSEVELT

WILLIAM WILLIAMS

15

MAKING THE JOURNEY TO AMERICA

Preparing for the journey to America took a long time. Immigrants often had to work day and night to save money for their passage. Some borrowed money from relatives. Others sold almost everything they owned. Often, families were separated for years at a time so that fathers, husbands, and brothers could work in America and send money home to support their families and save up for their relatives' tickets overseas.

At the turn of the century, an adult ticket on a steamship across the Atlantic Ocean cost about $35. Some Europeans fled their home countries because they were being treated badly. Others fled due to low economic activity, unemployment, and political opposition. To get to the steamship that would carry them across the Atlantic Ocean, many immigrants had to travel for months on foot or by wagon, train, boat, and ship.

IMMIGRANTS OFTEN TRAVELED IN STEERAGE, THE LOWEST CLASS OF **ACCOMMODATIONS** ON BOARD THE STEAMSHIPS. STEERAGE WAS A LARGE, CROWDED ROOM BELOW DECK WHERE THE WOMEN AND CHILDREN WERE SEPARATED FROM THE MEN BY A BLANKET HUNG OVER A ROPE THAT DIVIDED THE ROOM DOWN THE CENTER.

STEERAGE PASSENGERS GETTING FRESH AIR

17

ARRIVING AT ELLIS ISLAND

Steamship captains were required to provide passenger manifests, or lists, which stated the particulars of each immigrant. When creating these manifests, ticket agents would do a brief inspection of the immigrants. This was because steamship companies had to pay for the return tickets of immigrants who weren't allowed into America. Immigrants who weren't likely to be allowed into America weren't allowed to buy tickets.

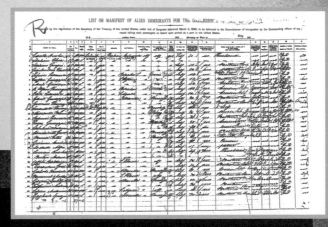

Sources from the Past

Immigrant manifests helped keep track of passengers aboard steamships and helped organize immigrants once they reached Ellis Island. These manifests are considered primary sources because they're written works from the time period being studied. The information on these manifests could help identify each passenger and decide whether they were fit to enter the United States. In addition to noting whether an immigrant was married and what their job was, manifests also included the person's medical information.

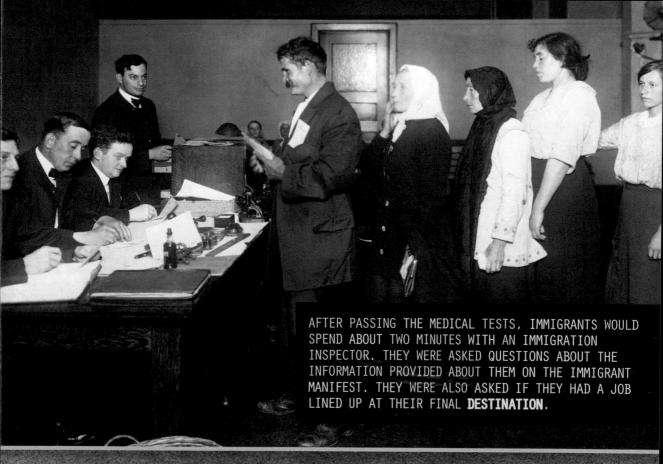

AFTER PASSING THE MEDICAL TESTS, IMMIGRANTS WOULD SPEND ABOUT TWO MINUTES WITH AN IMMIGRATION INSPECTOR. THEY WERE ASKED QUESTIONS ABOUT THE INFORMATION PROVIDED ABOUT THEM ON THE IMMIGRANT MANIFEST. THEY WERE ALSO ASKED IF THEY HAD A JOB LINED UP AT THEIR FINAL **DESTINATION**.

When immigrants arrived at Ellis Island, they underwent a medical screening. While waiting in line, their behavior and appearance were secretly observed to identify any outward signs of disease or disability. At the end of the long line, a doctor looked closely at each immigrant. Special attention was paid to their eyes, hands, and throat, where signs of illness could be detected.

DETAINED ON ELLIS ISLAND

It was common for immigrants to be detained, or held back, on Ellis Island for a number of reasons. They were most often detained because of money. Many immigrants weren't permitted to leave the island and enter the United States until they could prove they wouldn't become dependent on government services or private charity. About 20 percent of all arrivals were detained for a short time. Of those detained, only a small percentage were eventually kept separate and deported, or sent back to their country of origin.

Being detained on the island was often unpleasant, especially during the station's busiest years, between 1901 and 1914. Immigrants were packed into hospital sections or locked dormitories, or sleeping areas. The dormitories were crowded and full of lice. Detained immigrants met several times each day to eat, but were otherwise left to entertain themselves.

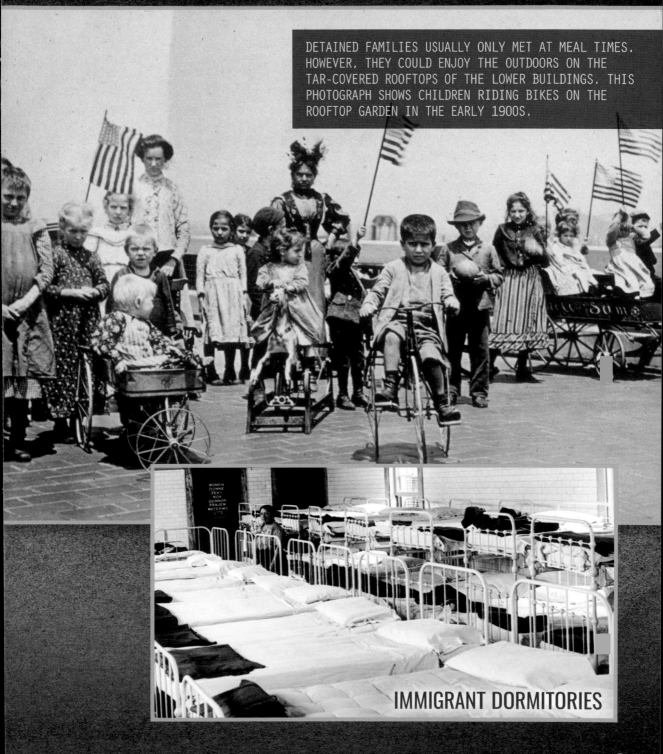

DETAINED FAMILIES USUALLY ONLY MET AT MEAL TIMES. HOWEVER, THEY COULD ENJOY THE OUTDOORS ON THE TAR-COVERED ROOFTOPS OF THE LOWER BUILDINGS. THIS PHOTOGRAPH SHOWS CHILDREN RIDING BIKES ON THE ROOFTOP GARDEN IN THE EARLY 1900S.

IMMIGRANT DORMITORIES

JUST THE BEGINNING

For many immigrants, beginning a new life in the United States wasn't easy. Life in the cities of America was much different than what they were used to in their home countries.

Immigrants of all nationalities and from all walks of life faced **discrimination** and hostility. Many lived in poor conditions in crowded tenements, or apartment buildings, that lined the streets of **ethnic** neighborhoods. Thousands of immigrants labored long hours in the dangerous working conditions found in the poorer parts of major cities.

Many immigrants dealt with the challenges of their new life by seeking comfort in their peoples' **traditions**. They joined ethnic groups of people, read newspapers in their language, and didn't stray far from their new neighborhoods where many people from their home country also lived.

TENEMENT BUILDINGS WERE CROWDED, SOMETIMES WITH UP TO 12 ADULTS CRAMPED INSIDE A SINGLE ROOM. MOST TENEMENT HOUSING DIDN'T HAVE RUNNING WATER OR INDOOR TOILETS.

IMMIGRATION SLOWS DOWN

With the outbreak of World War I in July 1914, immigration to the United States slowed down greatly. When the United States entered the war in April 1917, Ellis Island was turned into a holding center for 2,000 German prisoners of war (POWs). The POWs were mainly the crews of German ships docked in New York Harbor. Immigrants who were accused of committing various crimes were often held at Ellis Island with the German POWs.

IN 1918, THE GERMAN POWS WERE SENT TO HOLDING
CAMPS ELSEWHERE IN THE UNITED STATES.

In spring 1917, a new immigration law went into effect. This new law labeled 32 groups of immigrants as undesirable. The passage of this law signaled to the world that America was closing its borders. Soon, Ellis Island became a military headquarters, and most immigration inspections happened aboard ships.

A CHANGE OF ATTITUDE

After World War I ended, interest in immigration increased once again. However, Americans had grown less interested in welcoming immigrants to the United States. Many Americans came to distrust foreigners, whom they blamed for the recent war. Just before the war had ended, Congress passed a law that made it much easier to deport any immigrant suspected of being an **anarchist** or a **Communist**. Many of those being deported passed through Ellis Island on their way back to Europe.

BY THE 1920S, THE BUILDINGS ON ELLIS ISLAND WERE FALLING APART. MANY IMMIGRANTS SLEPT ON BLANKETS ON THE FLOOR BECAUSE THERE WEREN'T ENOUGH BEDS.

Sources from the Past

This image of the dormitory in Ellis Island hospital was taken in 2012. Does that make it a primary source? If not, is it still valuable to people studying the past? Why or why not?

Even though Americans didn't always welcome immigrants, by 1920, the number of new arrivals began to increase. Now, immigrants underwent more thorough medical examinations, and their baggage and clothing had to be cleaned to prevent the spread of disease. However, by this time, Ellis Island was falling apart and was in great need of repairs.

NEW LAWS

A series of public concerns made Congress reconsider immigration laws, and the First Quota Act took effect on June 3, 1921. This law stated that each foreign country would be allowed only a certain number of immigrants to be admitted to the United States. This made it very hard for many hopeful European immigrants to make a new life in America.

In spring 1924, Congress passed the Second Quota Act, which further limited the number of immigrants allowed into the country. Immigration at Ellis Island was sharply reduced as a result of the Second Quota Act.

Soon after the Second Quota Act was passed, medical examiners and immigration inspectors were employed at the U.S. government offices overseas to "preprocess" hopeful immigrants. This made the process at Ellis Island unnecessary.

THE NUMBER OF NEW IMMIGRANTS FROM ANY GIVEN COUNTRY ALLOWED BY THE FIRST QUOTA ACT WAS EQUAL TO 3 PERCENT OF THE POPULATION OF THAT NATIONALITY LIVING IN THE UNITED STATES DURING THE 1910 CENSUS. A CENSUS IS WHEN GOVERNMENT OFFICIALS COUNT THE NUMBER OF PEOPLE IN A COUNTRY, CITY, OR TOWN. CENSUS INFORMATION CAN BE A PRIMARY SOURCE, TOO.

Sources from the Past

This is a copy of the bill that eventually became the First Quota Act. Copies of original documents are still considered primary sources. What do you think we can learn from the copy of this bill? Why is it worthwhile to study things like this?

Desk Copy

Union Calendar No. 2.

67TH CONGRESS,
1ST SESSION.

H. R. 4075.

[Report No. 4.]

Mr. Oorkne

IN THE HOUSE OF REPRESENTATIVES.

APRIL 18, 1921.

Mr. JOHNSON of Washington introduced the following bill; which was referred to the Committee on Immigration and Naturalization and ordered to be printed.

APRIL 19, 1921.

Reported with amendments, committed to the Committee of the Whole House on the state of the Union, and ordered to be printed.

[Omit the part struck through and insert the part printed in italic.]

A BILL

To limit the immigration of aliens into the United States.

1   *Be it enacted by the Senate and House of Representa-*
2 *tives of the United States of America in Congress assembled,*
3   That as used in this Act—
4   The term " United States " means the United States

Amendment offered by Mr. Mann

OK

Page 1, line 6   *OK*

After the word _____ " _____ "

Strike out → "*Isthmian*"
Insert

29

A LINK TO HISTORY

After the Great Depression and World War II, Ellis Island no longer served as an immigration station. It closed its doors in 1955 and remained abandoned until May 11, 1965, when President Lyndon B. Johnson officially made it part of the Statue of Liberty National Monument. Reconstruction of Ellis Island began in 1984.

On September 10, 1990, the Ellis Island Immigration Museum opened to the public. In 2015, it was renamed the Ellis Island National Museum of Immigration. A trip to the museum offers a bridge to the past for many Americans whose relatives came to the United States as immigrants. Today, around 3 million people visit Ellis Island each year to see what life was like for people passing through the immigration station so long ago.

GLOSSARY

abuse: To treat or use something in a wrong or unfair way.

accommodations: A place where travelers can sleep and find other services.

anarchist: A person who goes against any authority, established order, or ruling power.

cholera: A serious disease that causes severe vomiting and diarrhea and that often results in death.

communist: A person who believes in or is a member of a political party that supports communism, which is a social system or theory in which property and goods are held in common.

destination: A place to which a person is going or something is being sent.

discrimination: Different—usually unfair—treatment based on factors such as a person's race, age, religion, or gender.

diverse: Made up of people or things that are different from each other.

ethnic: Of or relating to races or large groups of people who have the same customs, religion, or origin.

immigrant: A person who comes to a country to live there.

prejudice: An unfair feeling of dislike for a person or group because of race or religious or political beliefs.

tradition: A way of thinking, behaving, or doing something that's been used by people in a particular society for a long time.

INDEX

WEBSITES

Due to the changing nature of Internet links, PowerKids Press has developed an online list of websites related to the subject of this book. This site is updated regularly. Please use this link to access the list: www.powerkidslinks.com/eohs/ellis